Original title:
Lasting Love: Secrets to Longevity in Relationships

Copyright © 2024 Swan Charm
All rights reserved.

Author: Aron Pilviste
ISBN HARDBACK: 978-9916-89-112-4
ISBN PAPERBACK: 978-9916-89-113-1
ISBN EBOOK: 978-9916-89-114-8

Whispers of Infinity

Stars align in silent night,
Echoes dance in silver light.
Voices lost in timeless seas,
Whisper truths on cosmic breeze.

Galaxies in spiral twine,
Promises in fate entwine.
Infinite tales yet to see,
Wonders held in mystery.

Dreams awaken in the dark,
Flickers of a hidden spark.
Journey vast, the heart we chase,
In the void, we find our place.

Connections Carved in Stone

Ancient trees with roots so deep,
Stories shared that shadows keep.
Whispers echo through the years,
In the silence, strength appears.

Mountains rise with tales profound,
Carved in earth, their truths surround.
Footprints left on timeless trails,
In each step, the spirit sails.

Memory like rock withstands,
Holds our dreams in weathered hands.
Bonded hearts in clay and fire,
Crafting hopes that never tire.

A Path of Light

Morning breaks with gentle hue,
Promises of skies so blue.
Steps we take upon this ground,
In our hearts, the light is found.

Winding trails through forest vast,
Shadows linger but won't last.
Every turn a story told,
In the warmth, our dreams unfold.

Stars will guide our weary feet,
Radiance in every beat.
Onward through the darkest night,
Together, we will find the light.

Cradle of Understanding

In the quiet whispers we share,
A gentle bond without compare.
Hearts entwined in sacred space,
Finding solace in each embrace.

In the silence, truths are found,
A deeper love, forever bound.
Through the storms and sunlit days,
In understanding, love always stays.

The Bridges We Build

Across the rivers of our dreams,
We find a way through winding seams.
Each step taken, a path defined,
In every heartbeat, love aligned.

With every plank, our past laid bare,
Strength in unity, we both share.
Together, we rise above the fray,
Building bridges, come what may.

Moonlight and Memories

Beneath the glow of silver light,
We weave our tales through endless night.
Each memory, a star that gleams,
In the fabric of our dreams.

Laughter dances on the breeze,
Whispers soft, like rustling leaves.
With every moment, shadows fade,
In the moonlight, love is made.

The Rhythm of Us

In every heartbeat, a pulse we share,
The rhythm of us, a harmonious air.
Through highs and lows, we find our song,
In the dance of life, we both belong.

With every step, a story unfolds,
A melody sweet, as love's truth holds.
Together we sway, come rain or shine,
In the music of life, your heart and mine.

The Quilt of Experience

Each patch a story sewn with care,
Stitched together, joys and despair.
Colors blend, both dark and light,
A tapestry of life, woven tight.

Memories linger like a gentle thread,
In corners where the laughter spread.
Faded hues of years gone past,
Embracing moments, forever cast.

With each fold, a lesson learned,
In the warmth, the heart has yearned.
A pattern grows, intricate and wise,
In the quilt of life, knowledge lies.

Seasons change, yet it remains,
A stitched embrace through joy and pains.
Each square a lifetime, bright and bold,
Stories of the young, and tales of old.

In the quiet, one can find,
Reflections of a journey, intertwined.
The quilt of experience, richly spun,
A map of the heart, where all are one.

Candlelight Conversations

Flickering flames in the dim-lit room,
Whispers of secrets dispel the gloom.
Eyes meet softly, hearts entwined,
Words dance lightly, thoughts unconfined.

A gentle glow warms the night,
Embers flicker, spirits take flight.
With every laugh, the shadows sway,
In candlelight, worries drift away.

Old stories shared, anew they gleam,
A tapestry woven of hopes and dreams.
Laughter echoes, stories unfold,
In the warmth of the light, memories hold.

The world outside fades into the past,
In this sacred hour, moments amassed.
Each flicker tells a tale so sweet,
Candlelight conversations, where souls meet.

As the evening wanes, the light will dim,
But the bond we forge will never thin.
In whispered voices, truth remains,
Candlelight conversations, love unchains.

Footprints on the Sand

Waves crash gently upon the shore,
Each step a whisper, memories soar.
With every print a tale is spun,
Footprints on the sand, a day well done.

The tide rolls in, erasing the trails,
Yet the heart remembers, love prevails.
Sunset paints the sky in gold,
Stories of adventure quietly told.

With laughter echoing in the breeze,
Footprints dance among the seas.
Sweet moments caught in salty air,
A journey shared, a bond so rare.

As the stars begin to gleam,
I walk alone, lost in a dream.
Each grain of sand, a fleeting glance,
Footprints fade, yet hearts advance.

Through life's tides, we leave our mark,
A journey lit by joy's bright spark.
Though washed away, the love expands,
Forever cherished, our footprints on the sands.

Sacred Spaces

Nestled corners where silence reigns,
Whispers of nature soothe all pains.
In every breath, a calm embrace,
Within these walls, find sacred space.

The hum of stillness fills the air,
Heartbeats echo, a rhythm rare.
Memories linger, softly trace,
In quietude, we find our place.

Books stacked high, each page a door,
Stories waiting, wisdom to explore.
In the gentle light, dreams interlace,
Creating moments, a sacred space.

The mat beneath invites us to pause,
In meditation, we find our cause.
With each inhalation, doubts erase,
In the calmness, we seek grace.

Through daily chaos, return we must,
To sacred spaces, our hearts we trust.
In the stillness, the world we face,
A journey inward, in sacred space.

Beneath the Surface

In shadows deep, secrets weave,
The ocean's heart, so hard to perceive.
Ripples of truth, buried low,
Whispers of time, the currents flow.

Diving into depths unknown,
A world beneath, so overgrown.
Creatures dance, in silent grace,
They hold the tales, of every place.

Light filters through, a haunting glow,
Casting dreams, on waves below.
The water sways, a gentle hum,
Echoes of all, that we become.

So let us wander, hand in hand,
Exploring depths, not just the sand.
For beneath the surface, life thrives,
A hidden realm, where magic survives.

With every dive, we find our core,
A universe, forever to explore.
Beneath the waves, let's take our flight,
In the depths, we'll find our light.

Sails of Shared Dreams

In the twilight's soft embrace,
We set our course, a sacred place.
With sails unfurled, hearts in sync,
Crafting journeys on the brink.

Waves of hope beneath our feet,
Whispers of fate, a rhythmic beat.
Together we sail, through night and day,
Guided by stars that light the way.

Each gust of wind, a laughter shared,
In unison, our souls declared.
The horizon beckons, wide and vast,
With sails of dreams, we're free at last.

Storms may rise, we'll stand as one,
Through darkest nights, till morning's sun.
Hand in hand, we'll brave the tide,
On this voyage, love is our guide.

With every harbor, stories bloom,
Our hearts entwined, dispelling gloom.
So let's set forth, on this grand scheme,
Forever sailing, on shared dreams.

Conversations at Dusk

As daylight fades and shadows grow,
We gather close, in twilight's glow.
With whispered words, we paint the night,
Conversations soft, with gentle light.

Stories linger, memories shared,
In every glance, a heart laid bare.
Secrets bloom, like flowers in spring,
In quiet hours, love takes wing.

Stars begin to twinkle bright,
Illuminating what feels right.
With every laugh, and subtle sigh,
We find our truth, as time slips by.

The moon takes stage, a silver muse,
In this realm, we cannot lose.
Our voices rise, in harmony's song,
In these moments, we belong.

So let us linger, in the dusk,
Where words flow sweet, like fragrant musk.
In gentle twilight, our souls align,
In conversations deep, your heart is mine.

The Alchemy of Us

In the crucible of time and care,
We forge our bonds, a love laid bare.
With every touch, a spell we cast,
Turning moments into a vibrant past.

Your laughter twinkles, gold and bright,
Transforming shadows into light.
Alchemy flows, in rhythms sweet,
Together, we rise, on love's heartbeat.

Through trials faced, we learn and grow,
Mixing dreams, as a river flows.
With every tear, a gem we glean,
In the furnace of life, our vision seen.

So let's create, with hearts ablaze,
Silver linings in life's maze.
In the alchemy of us, we find,
A masterpiece, uniquely defined.

Transcending space, where secrets lie,
Our souls entwined, like stars on high.
Forever crafting, this bond we trust,
In the magic born, the alchemy of us.

Roots Deepened in Shared Soil

In the garden where we stand,
Our roots entwine beneath the sand.
Nurtured by the sun and rain,
Together we embrace the pain.

Seasons change, but we remain,
Holding fast through joy and strain.
In this earth, our stories grow,
A tapestry of love to show.

When the storms of life arrive,
We find the strength to survive.
Deepened roots, our bond is wide,
Forever standing side by side.

As we flourish, side by side,
In this soil, our hopes reside.
A legacy of love we sow,
In the shadows, our hearts glow.

With every leaf that starts to fall,
We find comfort in our call.
Roots that deepen, love that soars,
In this garden, forever yours.

The Light of Two Hearts Alight

In the twilight, our hearts ignite,
A beacon shining, oh so bright.
With every glance, the world fades away,
In your warmth, I long to stay.

Stars align in the evening sky,
Together, we learn to fly.
Two flames dancing in the dark,
A gentle whisper, love's sweet spark.

In laughter and tears, we find our way,
Through valleys dark and brightened day.
United, we face what comes our way,
With hands held tight, we'll never sway.

As the dawn breaks, we greet the morn,
In your light, my soul is reborn.
Together, a journey we embark,
Two hearts alight, igniting the spark.

With every heartbeat, promises flow,
A timeless bond that will only grow.
Together, forever, in love's gentle flight,
In the tapestry of life, we are the light.

Invisible Bonds that Tie the Soul

In silence, we share the weight of dreams,
Invisible threads weave softly it seems.
A glance, a touch, a knowing sigh,
In the quiet moments, we learn to fly.

Like whispers carried on the breeze,
Our spirits dance with effortless ease.
Unseen connections, strong and true,
In every heartbeat, I feel you.

Through the chaos, we find our calm,
With every challenge, we weave our balm.
Threads of fate, a tapestry spun,
In this story, we are one.

Distance may stretch, but never divide,
In the depths of my heart, you reside.
Invisible bonds that time can't sever,
In our souls, we are forever.

In the night sky, where wishes bloom,
I feel your presence in every room.
These invisible ties, a sacred pact,
In love's embrace, that's where we act.

A Symphony of Hearts in Tune

In the chorus of life, our hearts blend,
Each note a promise, love to send.
Together, we find our perfect key,
In harmony's embrace, wild and free.

Every heartbeat is a drum that plays,
In this rhythm, our spirits sway.
Melodies weave through the day and night,
In this symphony, our love takes flight.

The crescendos rise, the echoes fall,
Through every challenge, we hear the call.
In the encore of our days, we find,
A perfect union, beautifully aligned.

With every lyric, our story grows,
In verses written with love that glows.
Together, we compose the sweetest tune,
A symphony of hearts that swoon.

In the silence, we still hear the song,
Melodies binding us ever strong.
As the world plays on, we'll stay in tune,
A timeless rhythm beneath the moon.

Rooted in Respect

In the garden where we stand,
Bound by trust, hand in hand.
Roots entwined beneath the ground,
In our hearts, respect is found.

Through storms that shake and winds that blow,
We nurture seeds of care that grow.
With every laugh, with every tear,
Respect will flourish year by year.

As seasons change and time goes on,
Our bond, like vines, will carry on.
In silence shared and spoken word,
A melody of trust is heard.

Nature whispers, it gently shows,
The deeper roots, the stronger grows.
In every challenge we embrace,
We cultivate our sacred space.

So let us stand, not far apart,
With open minds and open heart.
United here, both rich and blessed,
In this life, we are rooted in respect.

Fire of Fidelity

In the hearth where hearts ignite,
Fidelity burns, warm and bright.
Through darkest nights, it lights the way,
A steadfast flame that will not sway.

In whispers soft, in vows we share,
A promise made, we're aware.
Through trials faced and winds that moan,
In this fire, we find our home.

Embers glow, our spirits rise,
In each other, we recognize.
The warmth we feel, it binds us close,
A testament that love's engrossed.

As branches bend, as storms may strike,
Fidelity's flame will stand alike.
In moments sweet and days of strife,
Our faithful love ignites our life.

So stoke the fire, let it blaze,
In the light of love, we'll always stay.
Through flames of time, our bond's displayed,
In the fire of fidelity, we're unafraid.

The Ironclad Bond

With every challenge, hand in hand,
We forge together, strong we stand.
An ironclad bond, unbreakable,
In this unity, we find our whole.

Through the heat of conflict's flame,
Our trust, unwavering, stays the same.
In trials faced, we learn and grow,
Together, we let our true strength show.

Like steel that's tempered in the fire,
Our hearts unite, we will inspire.
In silence shared and battles fought,
Through every struggle, we are taught.

In laughter bright and tears of grace,
We carry each other, no time to waste.
In every heartbeat, we find our song,
The ironclad bond where we belong.

So let the world challenge our might,
Together, we'll stand, ready to fight.
With open hearts, our spirits donned,
In this journey, we are the ironclad bond.

Mirrored Souls

In the depths of our shared gaze,
We find reflections, a wondrous maze.
Mirrored souls, entwined as one,
A journey begins, never to shun.

In laughter's echo and midnight's sigh,
Our spirits dance under the sky.
Each heartbeat shared, a rhythm aligned,
In the tapestry of love, intertwined.

Through shifting sands and twilight's hue,
Mirrored dreams unfold, bright and true.
In every glance, a story told,
With every touch, we're rich and bold.

As moments pass like drifting leaves,
In each other's warmth, our hope believes.
Two souls reflected, glowing bright,
In the gentle hush of the night.

So let us cherish this bond we hold,
In mirrored love, we'll always be told.
With open hearts, may we remain,
In this dance of souls, free from pain.

The Joy of Simple Moments

In the morning light, we laugh,
Coffee cups warm in our hands.
The world outside feels still,
Every moment, a treasure we've planned.

Walking barefoot on soft grass,
Chasing shadows in the sun.
Finding joy in quiet whispers,
Where silence and smiles are one.

A gentle breeze through the trees,
Birds singing sweet melodies.
With every breath, we feel alive,
In these moments, we are free.

The sun dips low, painting the sky,
Colors blend in a perfect array.
Hand in hand, we stand and sigh,
Grateful for this beautiful day.

As stars emerge and night unfolds,
We share stories and dreams anew.
In the joy of these simple moments,
Our hearts know love shines through.

Letters Never Sent

On parchment, words softly flow,
Thoughts and feelings laid bare.
But whispers die in the shadows,
Letters never sent, with care.

Promises hidden in ink,
Longing trapped in a line.
Each page holds a secret dream,
A heart's silent, aching sign.

The envelope waits, untouched,
Memories wrapped in doubt.
What if the words were released?
Could love bloom or fade out?

Time ticks on, the years move fast,
Yet the letters remain confined.
In dreams, I scream their names,
In silence, the truth, unkind.

One day, I might set them free,
A moment penned in light.
For now, I hold them close to me,
In shadows, they take flight.

Celestial Connections

Beneath the vast, starry dome,
We find our place in the night.
Hearts racing like comets,
In the darkness, we ignite.

We grasp at dreams and wishes,
Drawn to the moon's soft glow.
Each star a spark of hope,
In the cosmos, love does flow.

Planets dance in silent grace,
Orbits spinning, side by side.
In this universe, we embrace,
With every heartbeat, we guide.

Galaxies whisper ancient tales,
Of spirits meeting once more.
In the rhythm of the stars,
Connections that we can't ignore.

So we reach into the night,
Trust the path that lies ahead.
For in this vast expanse,
Celestial bonds are bred.

A Journey of Kindness

With every step, we share a smile,
A gesture small, yet bright.
In the warmth of kindness shared,
We kindle sparks of light.

A helping hand, a listening ear,
Together, we find our way.
Each moment spent in giving,
Turns darkness into day.

Words of comfort spoken true,
Lift spirits when they're low.
In the tapestry of life,
Kindness threads a vibrant glow.

Through valleys deep and mountains high,
We journey, heart to heart.
In the embrace of empathy,
We find our truest art.

So let us walk this path of grace,
With open hearts, we rise.
For in this journey of kindness,
We create a world that thrives.

The Flow of Forgiveness

In the river's gentle bend,
Resentments fade and mend.
Each ripple tells a tale,
Of love that will prevail.

A heart once cold and tight,
Releases in the light.
With every breath taken,
Old wounds no longer shaken.

Forgiveness flows like wine,
A nectar so divine.
With each sip, we renew,
A bond that feels so true.

Through tears, the pain dissolves,
Old grudges, now resolved.
We find our way back home,
In peace, no more to roam.

The heart, a canvas clear,
Painted bright, no fear.
Together, hand in hand,
We heal, a stronger band.

Crescendo of Commitment

In morning's quiet grace,
We find our rightful place.
With whispers soft and light,
Our hearts take flight tonight.

Promises wrapped in gold,
Stories waiting to be told.
Together, side by side,
In love, we find our pride.

Through valleys deep we walk,
In silence, we'll not talk.
Our souls in sync, they hum,
A beat, forever drum.

With every rising sun,
A new day has begun.
Our journey, vast and wide,
With faith, we will abide.

In laughter, in our tears,
We share our hopes and fears.
A symphony so grand,
Through life, we'll make our stand.

The Heart's Compass

In shadows, we find light,
A guide through darkest night.
The compass in our chest,
Points toward what is best.

With dreams that sail afar,
We follow every star.
Through storms that come our way,
Our hearts will not betray.

Each sigh, a whispered prayer,
In trust, we lay it bare.
The path will surely twist,
Yet love, we can't resist.

Through trials, we will grow,
As rivers ebb and flow.
Our north, a shining flame,
To love, we'll stake our claim.

With every step we take,
New memories we'll make.
Together, hand in hand,
Our hearts, a strong command.

Unspoken Promises

In silence, bonds are forged,
With glances, hearts are gorged.
Unspoken words resound,
In love, we are found.

A touch that lingers near,
Whispers only we hear.
In shadows, secrets dwell,
A story we won't tell.

Through time, a sacred trust,
In hearts, it's more than just.
Emotions softly weave,
In each other, we believe.

Our dreams, a shared refrain,
In joy, in loss, in pain.
The future glows ahead,
With every word unsaid.

As stars in night's embrace,
We find our rightful place.
In silence, love's decree,
A bond eternally.

The Art of Holding on

In shadows cast by doubt's embrace,
We find our strength, our steady pace.
With fragile hearts and dreams adorned,
We weave a tale of hope reborn.

Through trials faced, our spirits rise,
In whispered winds, love never lies.
With every breath, we mend and grow,
In tender bonds, we find our glow.

The warmth of hands that gently clasp,
Through fleeting moments, love's sweet grasp.
With each sunrise, our hearts entwine,
In sacred spaces, love will shine.

Together we will stand our ground,
In silent vows, our truth is found.
Through tears that fall, we learn to see,
The art of holding on, you and me.

As seasons change, we hold the thread,
With stories shared, as paths we tread.
Though storms may rage, our hearts are strong,
In the art of holding on, we belong.

Paths Intertwined

Two souls alike, yet worlds apart,
In whispered dreams, we share a start.
Through winding roads that twist and turn,
With every step, our hearts will yearn.

The laughter shared, the tears we shed,
In every word, the hope we've fed.
Together we will face the dawn,
Embracing life, our fears withdrawn.

Under starlit skies, we'll find a way,
With every night, we'll chase the day.
In gentle breezes, our whispers blend,
On this journey, love will never end.

The moments cherished, small and grand,
In silent prayers, we make our stand.
With open hearts, our stories twine,
As we walk on these paths aligned.

Through every storm, we hold the light,
In shadows cast, we find the bright.
Two paths converge, a fate combined,
In life's embrace, our souls aligned.

Weathering the Storms Together

When thunder roars and waters rise,
We find our shelter 'neath the skies.
With courage built from hearts that dare,
We weather storms, for we will share.

Through darkest nights, our spirits soar,
In every trial, we seek for more.
Hand in hand, we'll brave the rain,
Together strong, through joy and pain.

With every gust that shakes our ground,
Our love's a fortress, safe and sound.
In swirling winds, we'll find our way,
True hearts united, come what may.

In whispered words, we draw our breath,
With faith that conquers even death.
As lightning strikes, we'll stand so tall,
In storms together, we'll never fall.

So let the tempests come and go,
With warmth and strength, we'll face the flow.
In every storm, a bond we'll tether,
With hearts as one, we'll weather together.

Threads of Golden Hours

In moments shared beneath the sun,
With laughter bright, our hearts are won.
The golden hours, fleeting and rare,
Are woven tight in memories we share.

Through whispered dreams and echoes sweet,
Each thread connects, our lives complete.
In gentle light, our spirits dance,
With every glance, a second chance.

As sunlight fades into the night,
We hold these threads, our lives alight.
With every heartbeat, every sigh,
In golden moments, time won't die.

Among the stars that shine above,
We find the threads of endless love.
United in this tapestry,
The golden hours, just you and me.

So let us cherish every scene,
Within these threads, our hearts are seen.
In life's embrace, we stand and tower,
Forever marked by golden hours.

Ageless Affection

In the gentle light of dawn,
Our hearts beat soft and slow.
Whispers of a timeless bond,
In each moment, love will grow.

Years may pass, but still we share,
The warmth that we both know.
In every touch, a silent prayer,
That our love is free to flow.

Through seasons bright and dark,
We stand steadfast and true.
An ageless love, a sacred mark,
In everything we do.

With every laugh and tear we've shed,
The tapestry of us unfolds.
A thread of gold, where love is fed,
In stories that we've told.

So here we are, side by side,
With hearts that dance and sing.
In the depths of love we hide,
The joy that each day brings.

In the Garden of Us

In the garden where we meet,
Petals blush in silent grace.
Every moment feels complete,
In this sacred, lovely space.

Beneath the branches, hand in hand,
We weave dreams in sunlit air.
Two souls growing, life unplanned,
In a bond so rich and rare.

Each flower blooming tells our tale,
Of laughter, love, and gentle sighs.
Through every storm, we will not fail,
In harmony, our spirits rise.

The fragrance lingers in the breeze,
As we nurture what we've sown.
In soft whispers, hearts at ease,
Together, never alone.

As seasons change and time moves on,
We'll cherish every bloom.
In this garden, love's sweet song,
Forever lifts the gloom.

Love's Resilient Bloom

In the cracks of stone we find,
A flower breaking through the strife.
Love, in all its purest kind,
Holds the essence of our life.

Through winter's chill and summer's blaze,
We stand strong, our roots entwined.
In the light, love sets ablaze,
A fire that won't be confined.

Each challenge faced, a testament,
To the strength that flourishes here.
With every heartache, we consent,
To grow stronger year by year.

In every glance and soft embrace,
We find courage to endure.
Our love will always leave a trace,
Of resilience, strong and pure.

So let the storms come, let them howl,
We stand rooted, side by side.
In our hearts, we hear the call,
Of love's reign, our humble pride.

Secrets Woven in Silence

In the quiet of the night,
Moonlight dances on our skin.
We share secrets without fright,
In the stillness, love begins.

Each heartbeat speaks, a whisper soft,
Unraveled truths between us bloom.
Our souls soar high, our spirits loft,
In shadows cast within the room.

With every gaze, a silent thread,
We weave our dreams with care.
In the silence, words left unsaid,
Echo in the cool night air.

Beneath the stars, our stories blend,
A tapestry of heart and mind.
Secrets shared as we transcend,
In the love that we both find.

So hold my hand, in silence stay,
For in this space, we come alive.
With every heartbeat, come what may,
Our love will always thrive.

The Garden Where Love Grows

In the soil of tender dreams,
Petals bloom with bright desires,
Whispers dance beneath moonbeams,
Heartstrings pulled by nature's fires.

Sunlight spills on gentle leaves,
Each ray a promise softly told,
In this haven, joy believes,
Love's embrace, a treasure bold.

Raindrops kiss the thirsty ground,
Nurtured roots entwine below,
In the silence, peace is found,
Where emotions freely flow.

Butterflies drift, colors blend,
Nature's art in vibrant hues,
With every turn, a new friend,
In this garden, love renews.

Seasons change, yet still we stay,
Hand in hand through sun and rain,
Together strong, come what may,
In our hearts, love's sweet refrain.

Intertwined Destinies at Dawn

As the sun peeks o'er the hill,
Morning paints the sky in gold,
Two souls whisper, time stands still,
In these moments, love unfolds.

Footsteps trace a path anew,
Hand in hand, we find our way,
Every breath feels fresh and true,
Promises dance with the day.

Birds take flight, our spirits soar,
Chasing dreams that blend and shift,
In the silence, we explore,
Each heartbeat, a precious gift.

Together we face the unknown,
With a courage drawn from trust,
In the dawn, we've truly grown,
Crafting futures, bright and just.

As light breaks through the trees,
Our destinies entwined as one,
In this moment, love's a breeze,
Guiding us until we're done.

Unraveling the Mysteries of Us

In the quiet of the night,
Questions linger, shadows play,
Two hearts searching for the light,
In the depths where secrets lay.

With each glance, we catch a clue,
Unraveling the threads of fate,
In this dance, we learn anew,
What it means to love, to wait.

Words unspoken fill the air,
Revelations slowly bloom,
In the truth, we're stripped bare,
Finding solace in the room.

Time reveals the ties we share,
Through the storms and sunny skies,
In our journey, love's a flare,
Lighting up our hidden ties.

Every mystery, every fear,
We will face, and hand in hand,
Together, we will persevere,
Unraveling what we understand.

Illuminating the Path of Togetherness

With each step, we light the way,
Candles flicker with our dreams,
Through the dark, love's bright array,
Guiding us with gentle beams.

In the silence, we find peace,
Moments tender, soft and sweet,
With you, all my doubts cease,
In togetherness, we meet.

Every shadow, every turn,
Hand in hand, we face the night,
In our hearts, a constant burn,
Love's embrace, forever bright.

Amidst the chaos, we remain,
Two souls joined in every fight,
Through the joy and through the pain,
Together, we will find the light.

As the stars paint dreams above,
We will tread this path as one,
In the journey, we discover,
A life of love, forever spun.

Love's Mosaic

Each tile a memory, bright and unique,
Fragile hearts woven, tender yet bold.
In shadows and light, our colors speak,
A tapestry formed, worth more than gold.

Moments like whispers, softly they blend,
With laughter and tears, they dance through the years.
In every embrace, our stories ascend,
Creating a portrait of love without fears.

Together we shape this intricate art,
A journey of passion, of struggle and grace.
Each fragment a promise, a vow from the heart,
In the mosaic of life, we find our place.

Through storms and through sunshine, hand in hand,
We build and we nurture, never to part.
With each gentle touch, like grains of the sand,
We craft our forever, a love-filled chart.

So let us remember, in colors so bright,
Each piece tells a story, a love that won't fade.
In this beautiful chaos, we find our light,
Love's mosaic alive, forever handmade.

Between Every Breath

In silence we linger, time slips away,
Between every heartbeat, a world holds its sway.
A sigh filled with longing, a promise of peace,
In the midst of the noise, love finds its release.

Like whispers at twilight, secrets unfold,
In the pauses we cherish, a tale to be told.
Moments suspended, like stars in a sky,
In the breath of our hearts, together we fly.

With each gentle inhalation, dreams come alive,
A dance in the stillness, where hopes intertwine.
Through joy and through sorrow, we learn to survive,
In the space between breaths, our spirits align.

So speak with your silence, let feelings take flight,
In the rhythm of closeness, the heart finds its might.
For love is a language that needs not a sound,
In the depth of connection, our souls are unbound.

In this beautiful hush, where you and I meet,
Between every breath, our love is complete.
In the dance of existence, we find our own song,
For it's here in the stillness, we truly belong.

The Anchors We Choose

In tides of uncertainty, we hold on tight,
To anchors of trust, casting shadows of light.
Through tempests and trials, our bonds stay strong,
In the depths of the ocean, together we belong.

Each friendship a vessel, with sails made of care,
Navigating storms, our hearts bravely share.
With laughter like sails, we glide through the waves,
In the calm after chaos, our spirits are brave.

We gather the moments, like shells on the shore,
Collecting the memories, forever we store.
In the heart of the tempest, we never let go,
For the anchors we choose, endlessly grow.

Through fair winds and foul, in sunlight and rain,
We find in each other, both shelter and gain.
With every horizon, new journeys will call,
The anchors we choose, will conquer it all.

So let us set sail on this voyage of dreams,
With courage as compass, and love as our theme.
In the vastness of life, our souls are the crew,
In the anchors we choose, we forever renew.

Ceremonies of Togetherness

In gatherings shared, we find sacred space,
Ceremonies of love, smiles on each face.
With stories exchanged and laughter that flows,
We weave through the moments, a tapestry grows.

With candles ablaze, and hearts open wide,
We celebrate journeys, with joy as our guide.
In rituals old, and new ones we create,
Each heartbeat an echo, in love we relate.

As seasons keep turning, our bond only grows,
In the fabric of time, our togetherness shows.
Through dinners and dances, through tears and bright cheers,
These ceremonies circle, anchoring our years.

In the warmth of companionship, we gather near,
To honor the moments, to cherish and cheer.
With each thread of connection, we boldly declare,
In the shadows of doubt, we're always aware.

So let us be present, in this sacred embrace,
In the ceremonies shared, we find our true place.
For love is the thread that binds us with grace,
In togetherness blooming, we find our own space.

Unfading Hearts

In the twilight's soft whisper,
Love's warmth gently glows,
Hand in hand we wander,
Through time's endless flows.

Promises are woven,
In the fabric of dreams,
With each heartbeat echoing,
Life's delicate themes.

Seasons may change,
But we stay the same,
In the depths of our souls,
Burns an eternal flame.

Through shadows and sunlight,
Together we stand,
Anchored in each other,
As we traverse this land.

In laughter and tears,
In moments we share,
Unfading hearts,
Bound by love's gentle care.

Embrace of Eternity

In the silence where echoes,
Of whispers reside,
We find our forever,
With nothing to hide.

Stars twinkle above,
In the vastness of night,
Guiding our journey,
With shimmering light.

The moon softly cradles,
Our dreams in her glow,
In this dance of existence,
Together we flow.

With each fleeting moment,
Time stands still,
In the embrace of eternity,
Our hearts learn to feel.

Through whispers of starlight,
And shadows that play,
We cherish this bond,
In love's grand ballet.

From Seeds to Seasons

Beneath the rich soil,
Tiny seeds start to grow,
Reaching for the sun,
In a radiant show.

Through spring's gentle touch,
Life bursts into bloom,
Colors dance freely,
Chasing away gloom.

With summer's warm kiss,
Fruits hang ripe and bright,
Harvesting joy,
In the sweet golden light.

As autumn leaves fall,
We prepare for the night,
With hope in our hearts,
For tomorrow's new light.

In winter's cold grasp,
Quietude takes hold,
From seeds to seasons,
Life's story unfolds.

The Dance of Grace

In a world of hurried steps,
We find a slower pace,
Every movement whispers,
The dance of grace.

With gentle hands guiding,
And hearts open wide,
We twirl like the leaves,
With the breeze as our guide.

In laughter and rhythm,
Our souls intertwine,
With each sway and turn,
Our spirits align.

Through trials and triumphs,
We learn to embrace,
The beauty in balance,
In this wondrous space.

For life's a grand ballet,
With partners we face,
Together we flourish,
In the dance of grace.

A Tapestry of Trust

In threads of gold, we weave our fate,
A bond unspoken, yet so innate.
Through trials faced, side by side,
In every moment, love's gentle tide.

Each word like silk, each promise pure,
In every glance, our hearts ensure.
Together we'll stand, come what may,
Trust in our hearts, lighting the way.

Through tangled paths, we find our way,
With hands entwined, there's hope to sway.
In every laugh, in every tear,
A tapestry woven, forever near.

As seasons change, so does our thread,
But through it all, our love is spread.
In the fabric of life, we find our place,
A tapestry rich, woven with grace.

In the darkest night, we find our light,
A guiding star, burning bright.
In the threads of trust, we forever bind,
A love so deep, eternally kind.

Heartbeats in Harmony

In sync we move, two hearts as one,
A silent dance, under the sun.
With every beat, a story told,
In rhythms old, our love unfolds.

The whispers soft, a gentle breeze,
In perfect time, our souls at ease.
With every glance, a sweet embrace,
In this heartbeat, we find our place.

Through storms that rage, we stay aligned,
In harmony's song, our spirits twined.
With breaths in sync, the world fades away,
Our hearts will guide, come what may.

Within this bond, we find our peace,
In love's soft rhythm, all worries cease.
Together we sing, a joyful refrain,
In heartbeats true, there's no more pain.

As time moves on, our melody stays,
In every moment, love's sweet displays.
With hearts united, forever we'll be,
In harmony's embrace, eternally free.

Love's Enduring Glow

In the twilight's gleam, our spirits soar,
A flame ignites, forevermore.
With whispers soft, the night unfolds,
In love's embrace, a tale retold.

Through fading light, we stand as one,
In shadows cast, our hearts still run.
With every spark, our passions grow,
In love's embrace, an enduring glow.

Against the night, our love will shine,
A beacon bright, forever mine.
With each caress, the stars align,
In endless love, our fates entwine.

Through every storm, our light remains,
In tender words, and gentle strains.
With courage found, we face the cold,
In love's warmth, worth more than gold.

As seasons pass, our hearts will know,
Through every change, we'll ebb and flow.
In the dusk of life, our fire's aglow,
In love's embrace, an endless flow.

In the Cadence of Time

Time whispers softly, a gentle tune,
In the still of night, beneath the moon.
Each moment counts, a ticking clock,
In every second, our hearts unlock.

As hours pass, we dance and sway,
With every step, we find our way.
In laughter shared, in silence found,
In the cadence of time, love's profound.

Through fleeting days, we hold on tight,
With dreams in sight, we chase the light.
In twilight's glow, we pause and reflect,
In every sigh, our souls connect.

From dawn to dusk, our journey runs,
In moments cherished, like setting suns.
In the fabric woven, we find our rhyme,
In the dance of life, the cadence of time.

As seasons turn, we do not fear,
With hands held close, our path is clear.
In every heartbeat, we find our climb,
In the rhythm of love, through the cadence of time.

Garden of Gentle Touches

In the garden, petals glow,
Whispers soft, like winds that flow.
Colors blend in warm embrace,
Nature's art, a tranquil space.

Breezes dance and gently sway,
Sunshine brightens every day.
Fingers trace the leaves so green,
Life unfolds, a sight unseen.

Butterflies in fleeting flight,
Chasing joy, their hearts alight.
Amidst the blooms, a secret song,
In this haven, we belong.

Raindrops kiss the thirsty ground,
In each droplet, magic found.
Roots run deep, connections strong,
In this realm, we all belong.

With each touch, a bloom we share,
Tender moments, free from care.
In this garden, hearts unite,
Guided by the softest light.

The Poetry of Patience

In silence, we learn to wait,
Time unfolds, revealing fate.
With each tick, a lesson found,
Seeds of hope, through trials bound.

Mountains rise, and rivers bend,
Every journey leads to mend.
Through the storms, we find our peace,
In the stillness, doubts release.

Let the clock's soft ticking sound,
Guide the heart, where dreams abound.
Moments stretch, then come to light,
In the calm, we find our sight.

Patience blooms like flowers rare,
In time's garden, tend with care.
Trust the process, let it be,
In the waiting, we are free.

For every struggle, every tear,
Leads us closer, year by year.
The poetry of life unfolds,
In each breath, a story told.

Winds of Change and Care

Gentle breezes start to blow,
Turning leaves in soft tableau.
With each gust, old ways depart,
New horizons spark the heart.

Voices whisper through the trees,
Telling tales with every breeze.
Embrace the shift, let go of fears,
In the winds, we dry our tears.

Nature's call, both strong and sweet,
Guides our steps, makes our hearts beat.
Change, a dance we learn to sway,
Through the night and into day.

Hands together, we will stand,
Facing storms, we make our plan.
With each breeze, let courage flare,
In the winds of change and care.

Hope rises in the skies so wide,
In the journey, know we stride.
Together we embrace the new,
With open hearts, we see it through.

Chasing Shadows Hand in Hand

In twilight's glow, we start to roam,
Chasing shadows, finding home.
With laughter light, we weave a tale,
In the dusk, where dreams set sail.

Hold my hand and take a leap,
Through the night, our secrets keep.
Every whisper, soft and clear,
Guiding paths that feel so near.

In the moonlight, shadows dance,
Stories born from sweet romance.
With every step, we find our way,
In the magic of the gray.

Trust the night, and let it guide,
Together, always by my side.
Through the mystery, we will tread,
Chasing shadows, hearts widespread.

With each moment, time expands,
Dreams take root in shifting sands.
Hand in hand, we find our light,
In the shadows, love ignites.

The Melody of Shared Dreams

In the stillness of the night,
Whispers dance in silver light.
Hearts entwined, we hold the key,
To unlock our destiny.

With every note of laughter sung,
Hope and joy alike are sprung.
In our hearts, a symphony,
Echoes of our unity.

Through fields of stars, we chase our fate,
Hand in hand, we navigate.
Woven threads of dreams aligned,
In this world, your heart is mine.

Beneath the vast and open sky,
Together, we will always fly.
In the chorus of our day,
Love will guide us on our way.

In the quiet, sweet embrace,
We find beauty, we find grace.
Together, we will always gleam,
In the melody of shared dreams.

Starlit Promises in Quiet Nights

In the hush of twilight's glow,
Promises made, softly flow.
Underneath the velvet sky,
Whispers linger, time goes by.

Glimmers of stars shine above,
Revealing secrets, tales of love.
In your eyes, the world is bright,
Guiding me through darkest night.

Moments shared, a sacred space,
Every heartbeat, every trace.
With starlit vows, we stand strong,
In this night where we belong.

Time may fade, yet we will stay,
Bound by dreams that light our way.
In the quiet, truth unfolds,
Journey written, love retold.

Through the shadows, we will dance,
Taking each and every chance.
With starlit promises in sight,
Love will guide us through the night.

Anchored in Each Other's Laughter

In the warmth of shared delight,
Laughter bubbles, pure and bright.
Tides of joy washing ashore,
With every chuckle, we want more.

Moments captured, floating clear,
Echoing memories we hold dear.
In your gaze, the world feels light,
Together, we create our flight.

Every giggle, every grin,
Shall be woven deep within.
In the storm, we find our peace,
Anchored hearts will never cease.

Laughter's harmony guides our way,
Through the night and into day.
Crafting joy in what we do,
Forever, I'll be here with you.

Each shared moment, a treasure found,
In laughter's arms, we are bound.
With every smile, we soar high,
Anchored in each other's sky.

The Pages of Our Enduring Story

Each page turned, a tale unfolds,
Whispers of the ages told.
In the chapters, love we trace,
Finding magic in this space.

With a pen of dreams, we write,
Illuminated by starlight.
Words like threads, entwined in time,
Together crafting every rhyme.

Through the twists and turns we roam,
In each other, we find home.
Every lesson, every fight,
Shapes our future, shines so bright.

In the tapestry of our days,
Painted in exquisite ways.
With every heartbeat, we explore,
The pages of our endless lore.

As the sun sets, our story glows,
Rooted deep, love surely grows.
In this book, we are aligned,
The pages vast, forever entwined.

Our Seasons of Change

Spring whispers softly, blooms arise,
Colorful petals kiss the skies.
Summer brings warmth, laughter, and light,
Days stretch long, fading into night.

Autumn's embrace, leaves turn to gold,
Stories of summer are gently told.
Winter descends, cloaked in white,
Silence wraps the world tight and bright.

Cycles repeat, a dance of time,
Nature's rhythm, a soothing rhyme.
With every season, we learn to grow,
Embracing the changes, steady and slow.

In fleeting moments, we find our peace,
Each season a chance for sweet release.
The heart learns to soar, the spirit to sway,
In the beauty of life, we find our way.

So let us honor the seasons' call,
In each bittersweet transition, we stand tall.
For in every ending, beginnings we find,
A tapestry woven, forever entwined.

Threads of Resilience

In the shadows, strength does spark,
A flame ignites, breaking the dark.
Woven together, stories unfold,
Tales of courage, both fierce and bold.

Through storms we weather, hearts hold true,
With every struggle, we learn anew.
Threads of hope, stitched with care,
We rise from ashes, breathing the air.

Unity binds us, hand in hand,
Together we conquer, together we stand.
In the face of trials, we bend, not break,
Resilience blooms, for our own sake.

With every challenge, a lesson we glean,
In the tapestry of life, each thread a dream.
Through the silence, our voices sing,
A chorus of strength, in unison we bring.

So let us cherish these threads we weave,
In the fabric of life, we all believe.
Together we forge a path ahead,
In every heartbeat, in every tread.

The Bridge of Vulnerability

Across the chasm, we build our bridge,
A span of trust, a gentle ridge.
With open hearts, we face our fears,
In vulnerability, we find our tears.

Each step taken, a leap of faith,
In shared moments, we find our place.
With every whisper, our souls lay bare,
In the soft light of truth, we find our care.

Fragile yet strong, like a spider's thread,
In tender spaces, our spirits spread.
Embracing the flaws, the scars we share,
In the bridge of connection, love fills the air.

So let us cross, hand in hand,
In the depths of being, together we stand.
For in the openness, we teem with grace,
In vulnerability's warmth, we find our space.

As hearts unlock and stories entwine,
The bridge we build becomes divine.
In every moment, every sigh,
Vulnerability soars, reaching the sky.

In Quietude We Thrive

In the stillness, whispers rise,
Nature's murmur, the heart replies.
Beneath the surface, life unfolds,
In silent moments, wisdom beholds.

Amidst the chaos, we seek our calm,
A gentle breath, a soothing balm.
In soft shadows, we find our way,
Guided by grace, come what may.

In quietude, our thoughts take flight,
Ideas bloom in the soft twilight.
As echoes linger, stillness reigns,
In peaceful pauses, clarity gains.

So let us dwell in serene embrace,
Finding solace in this sacred space.
In the hush of the night, dreams align,
In quietude, our souls intertwine.

Through silence, we awaken and grow,
In tranquil moments, we come to know.
In every heartbeat, in every sigh,
In quietude, we learn to fly.

Journeys of the Heart

Across the winding roads we tread,
With whispers soft, our spirits fed.
Each step a tale, each turn a dance,
In every heartbeat, there's romance.

Through valleys deep and mountains high,
We search for truth beneath the sky.
With open arms, we meet the light,
In shadows cast, we find our sight.

The rivers flow, they guide our way,
In night's embrace, we find our day.
With every tear, a lesson learned,
In every love, a fire burned.

So hold my hand, let's face the dawn,
With courage strong, we carry on.
For every journey, vast and wide,
We walk together, side by side.

In the end, it's love we trace,
The sweetest gift, our warm embrace.
Through every journey, heart to heart,
We'll never be alone, apart.

A Life in Bloom

In gardens rich, the colors sway,
Each petal holds a tale to say.
With sunlit grace, the flowers rise,
A fragrant dance beneath the skies.

The morning dew, a gentle kiss,
Awakens dreams we cannot miss.
With every bloom, new hopes ignite,
As seasons change, we find our light.

Beneath the shade of ancient trees,
The whispers weave upon the breeze.
In every bud, a promise waits,
With open hearts, we celebrate.

Through storms and winds, we face the fight,
With roots so deep, we claim our right.
To grow with love, wild and free,
A life in bloom, just you and me.

So cherish moments, let them last,
In every present, hold the past.
With each new dawn, our spirits soar,
In nature's song, we are much more.

Together in Silence

In quietude, our hearts align,
No words are needed, love divine.
With gentle breaths, we share our space,
In depths where time cannot erase.

A single glance, a knowing smile,
The world fades out, just for a while.
With fingers entwined, we find our peace,
In hushed connection, worries cease.

Through twilight's glow, we softly roam,
In serene stillness, we find home.
With every heartbeat, softly shared,
In unspoken bonds, we feel cared.

The stars above, they guide our way,
As moonlight dances, night turns day.
In silence deep, our spirits merge,
In every pause, our thoughts converge.

So let us cherish this sweet embrace,
In quiet moments, our sacred space.
Together in silence, strong and true,
With every whisper, it's me and you.

Echoes in Time

The past resounds in whispers clear,
With echoes that we hold so dear.
In memories bright, the shadows play,
While ghosts of yore gently sway.

Through corridors where silence breathes,
We find the truth that time bequeathes.
With every step, the years unwind,
In every pulse, our souls aligned.

The laughter lingers, the tears remain,
In woven tales of joy and pain.
With every heartbeat, stories bloom,
In timeless halls, dispelling gloom.

In every moment, reflections gleam,
As we chase shadows of a dream.
The future calls with voices old,
In echoes soft, our lives unfold.

So let us honor the paths we've crossed,
In every gain, we'll count the loss.
For echoes linger, clear and bright,
As we wade through the sea of night.

Beneath the Starlit Sky

Under the vast expanse we lay,
Counting stars that softly sway,
Whispers of dreams in the night,
Guided by the silver light.

The moon sings a lullaby sweet,
Echoes linger, a gentle beat,
With every breath, our hearts align,
In the stillness, love will shine.

Cool breeze carries secrets near,
In this moment, all is clear,
Hand in hand, we drift away,
Beneath the sky, where wishes play.

Time stands still, yet hearts race on,
As constellations paint our dawn,
With every glance, a spark ignites,
Beneath the starlit, endless nights.

Together here, we find our place,
In the cosmos, an endless space,
Bound by dreams that never die,
Forever lost, beneath the sky.

Fireflies and Promise

In the twilight, fireflies dance,
Casting light with every glance,
A soft glow in the evening air,
Whispers of hope, beyond compare.

Promises made under the trees,
Carried gently with the breeze,
Moments captured, fleeting yet bright,
In the realm of gentle night.

Laughter mingles with the sighs,
Stars twinkle in our hopeful eyes,
As shadows play upon the grass,
Time stands still, as dreams amass.

Together we weave stories bold,
In the warmth, when nights grow cold,
With every spark, love's light ignites,
In this dance of firefly nights.

Beneath the moon, we stand as one,
With hearts ablaze, our journey's begun,
In the whispers of dark, we find our way,
Fireflies and promise, guiding our stay.

Anchored in Togetherness

In the harbor, we find our peace,
Where tides of time gently cease,
Anchored firm in love's embrace,
Together we carve out our space.

Waves may crash, storms may arise,
But in each other, we see the skies,
With every challenge, hand in hand,
Side by side, we make our stand.

Sails unfurling, hearts set free,
Navigating life's vast sea,
In the stillness, we find our song,
Together, we always belong.

Moments shared, laughter and tears,
Woven tightly through all the years,
In this journey, we share the quest,
Anchored in love, we are truly blessed.

As the sun sets on distant shores,
With every dawn, our spirit soars,
In our harbor, love shines bright,
Anchored in togetherness, our guiding light.

The Canvas of Us

On this canvas, colors blend,
Each stroke speaks of love, our friend,
With every hue, a story told,
Of dreams we chase, of hearts of gold.

Brush dipped in passion, strokes so bold,
Capturing moments, never old,
With laughter ringing like a bell,
Underneath our shared carousel.

Canvas spreads beneath our feet,
Every memory, a joyful feat,
Blending shadows, light, and grace,
In this masterpiece, we find our place.

Patience paints the quiet nights,
As starlight dances, igniting sights,
Creating dreams that bloom anew,
The canvas of us, in every hue.

Together we craft, a life divine,
In every corner, your heart entwined,
With each brush stroke, love's enduring flame,
Forever and always, our hearts the same.

The Legacy of Us Through Time

We stand beneath the ancient trees,
Roots entwined in history's breeze.
Memories carved in bark and stone,
A legacy forged, never alone.

The echoes of laughter, soft and sweet,
Dance in the air where moments meet.
Each story passed from heart to heart,
A tapestry drawn, where we all start.

Time flows like the river's song,
A current where we all belong.
Threads of gold in the fabric weave,
Reminding us of love to believe.

Footprints on the path we share,
Guiding us through joy and care.
In every glance, in every sigh,
Our legacy whispers, never shy.

So let us write our tale anew,
With every breath, just me and you.
For in the end, through trials we strive,
It's the legacy of us that will survive.

Timeless Whispers

In twilight's glow, the stars align,
Whispers of love in every line.
Time spins softly, a silken thread,
Carrying dreams where angels tread.

Each moment captured in twilight's hue,
A gentle reminder of me and you.
Through ages past, our voices call,
In the silence, we hear it all.

The moonlit dances, shadows play,
Stories untold in shadows stray.
In every heartbeat, a promise made,
Timeless whispers that never fade.

So let the hours drift like sand,
Held tightly in each other's hand.
For in this world, both vast and wide,
We find our peace, where dreams reside.

Every soft note, a sweet refrain,
In the orchestra of joy and pain.
Together we'll weave, forever bound,
In timeless whispers, love profound.

Echoes of Forever

In the quiet dusk, a whisper stirs,
Echoes of forever, time concurs.
Through valleys low and mountains high,
Our spirits soar, our dreams comply.

With every sunset, our hearts entwine,
Bound by the stars in a cosmic design.
We chase the dawn, the day's embrace,
In echoes of forever, we find our place.

The softest breeze carries your name,
In every shadow, it's all the same.
Timeless moments, we hold them dear,
In the silence, your voice I hear.

Each gentle touch, a sacred trust,
In echoes of love, in dawn's soft rust.
We dance through time, two souls aglow,
In the fabric of forever, we cherish the flow.

So take my hand, let's wander wide,
In this journey, be my guide.
For with each heartbeat, our spirits soar,
In echoes of forever, we'll always explore.

The Thread That Binds

In every thread, a story we sew,
Colors of life in a vibrant flow.
The ties that bind through joy and strife,
A tapestry woven with love for life.

From laughter shared to tears embraced,
In every moment, our love is traced.
A journey crafted through time and space,
In the thread that binds, we find our grace.

Though storms may rage and shadows fall,
Together we'll rise, we won't enthrall.
For strength in numbers, in heart entwined,
In the thread that binds, true love we find.

Through seasons changing, we'll grow and bend,
In every chapter, we rise again.
For woven tightly, our spirits shine,
In the fabric of us, a love divine.

So let us cherish what we hold dear,
In every thread, we persevere.
For in this life, our souls aligned,
In the thread that binds, forever combined.

Navigating the Tides of Togetherness

In the silent whispers of dawn's light,
We sail through the waves, hearts in flight.
Hand in hand, we chart our course,
Fueled by love, our greatest source.

Through storms and calms, we hold tight,
Together we face the darkest night.
With every tide, our bond will grow,
In unity's strength, we'll always flow.

The horizon calls, a distant dream,
In every challenge, we'll find our seam.
With laughter and tears, we'll navigate,
Together we'll conquer, never too late.

Every sunrise brings promise anew,
With you by my side, I know we'll get through.
In the dance of time, we'll weave our fate,
Navigating life, together we'll create.

So here's to the journey, the paths we chose,
In the tapestry of life, our love brightly glows.
Through every tide that dares to test,
In togetherness, we find our rest.

The Dance of Enduring Hearts

In the rhythm of life, we find our song,
With every heartbeat, we learn to belong.
Side by side, we take the floor,
In the dance of love, we crave more.

With every challenge, we twirl and spin,
In the embrace of trust, we always win.
Our movements blended in perfect grace,
Enduring hearts, we set the pace.

Every step taken, a story unfolds,
In the warmth of your arms, I find my gold.
In the laughter and joy, in the tears we shed,
Together we dance, where dreams are led.

Through seasons that change and time that flies,
With you, my love, the world never lies.
In the dance of enduring hearts, we remain,
In every twirl, we find the same strain.

So here's to our waltz, forever refined,
In the layers of love, our spirits aligned.
With every move, our souls intertwine,
In this endless dance, forever you'll be mine.

Threads Woven in Shared Laughter

In the tapestry rich with colors bright,
Each thread a memory, woven tight.
Laughter rings in the heart of our days,
Filling the air in countless ways.

With joy that sparkles like the stars above,
We stitch our stories with laughter and love.
In every giggle, a bond secured,
In shared moments, our souls are cured.

From whispered jokes to playful schemes,
We weave the fabric of our dreams.
Each chuckle a thread in this vibrant weave,
In the warmth of our laughter, we truly believe.

Through all the seasons of life, come what may,
With threads of laughter, we light the way.
In the memories shared, our joy takes flight,
Woven together, we shine so bright.

So here's to the laughter, the joys we create,
With every shared smile, we celebrate fate.
In the quilt of existence, forever we stand,
Threads woven in laughter, hand in hand.

Cherished Echoes of a Shared Journey

In the echoes of time, our footsteps trace,
A journey together, a beautiful space.
With shared adventures and tales to tell,
In the heart of our story, we always dwell.

From dawn till dusk, hand in hand we roam,
In every moment, we build our home.
With cherished echoes that softly sing,
In the symphony of life, love is our string.

Through valleys low and mountains high,
Together we soar, reaching for the sky.
In every challenge, our spirits soar,
In the echoes of love, we always explore.

With memories that twinkle like stars at night,
We find our way, guided by light.
In the laughter shared and the tears we've cried,
Cherished echoes remind us, forever side by side.

So here's to our journey, paths intertwined,
In the fabric of time, our hearts designed.
With every echo, our love will stay,
In cherished moments, we'll find our way.

Eternal Threads of Togetherness

In the fabric of life, we weave,
Threads of laughter and gentle sighs,
Each moment stitched with care,
A tapestry of love that never dies.

Through storms and shadows, we stand tall,
With hands entwined, unbroken bond,
In the heart's quiet space we call,
A refuge where we both respond.

Every glance a silent vow,
Every heartbeat, a song that plays,
Together, we're anchored, here and now,
In the rhythm of our endless days.

With every season, our colors blend,
Bright hues of joy, soft shades of pain,
Together we rise, together we mend,
In the sunshine and the rain.

Forever may we walk this thread,
Eternal, strong, and true,
In every word we've ever said,
Our love remains, ever new.

Whispers of Time and Trust

In shadows, soft secrets lie,
With whispers carried on the breeze,
Time cradles moments, passing by,
Trust blooms gently between the trees.

Through the years, we share our tales,
Each heartbeat echoes with intent,
In silence, love's voice never fails,
With open hearts, we are content.

Fleeting hours become like gold,
In the tender light, we find our way,
Stories cherished, forever told,
In memories that never fray.

Beneath the stars, our dreams entwine,
A pattern carved by fate's own hand,
With every glance, our souls align,
In the vastness of this promised land.

Through time's embrace, we hold each other,
With trust as vast as the endless sky,
In this journey, you're my forever,
Our whispers soaring, flying high.

The Heart's Everlasting Embrace

In the soft glow of the evening light,
I find safety in your gentle gaze,
With every heartbeat, love takes flight,
An everlasting song that plays.

Through trials faced and joys we share,
In the quiet moments, our spirits meld,
In every hug, I feel you there,
A sanctuary where hope is held.

Your laughter dances in the air,
A melody that calms my mind,
In your arms, I am laid bare,
A refuge for two souls intertwined.

Together we rise, through thick and thin,
With strength we nurture, never bend,
In the tapestry of love we spin,
Our hearts forever, hand in hand.

With every dawn, a fresh embrace,
In the warmth of your love, I find rest,
Together we'll journey, with endless grace,
In the heart's ever-living quest.

Timeless Vows and Unspoken Words

Beneath the stars, a vow is made,
In the silence, promises bloom,
With every beat, foundations laid,
In the quiet, love finds room.

Through the chapters of our fate,
In laughter shared and tears that fall,
We navigate through all of hate,
In every challenge, we stand tall.

Unspoken words between our hearts,
A language only we can know,
In every look, our story starts,
A symphony of trust that flows.

With timeless grace, we journey on,
In moments cherished, breaths we take,
Together weaving dusk to dawn,
In every choice, the love we make.

Forever bound, our spirits soar,
In vow and trust, we bloom anew,
Through every day, we seek for more,
In timeless love, just me and you.

Ebb and Flow of Compassionate Currents

In twilight's soft embrace, we stand,
Waves of kindness, gentle hand in hand.
Hearts entwined within the tides,
Where love and hope forever resides.

Each ripple speaks of shared plight,
Listening close through the starry night.
Together we navigate the sea,
Casting nets of empathy.

The currents shift, they ebb and flow,
In silent whispers, we come to know.
For every heartache thus we share,
Compassion blooms, a faithful care.

As dawn breaks, we rise anew,
With every challenge, our bond grew.
In waves of laughter, in tears we shed,
We embrace the journey, hearts widespread.

Harmony flows like a melody sweet,
In every stumble, we find our feet.
United in purpose, we find our way,
Through the ebb and flow, day by day.

Fortresses Built on Trust and Kindness

In quiet corners, we lay our dreams,
Woven carefully, or so it seems.
With bricks of trust and beams of care,
We build a haven from the wear.

Each promise made, a solid stone,
In this fortress, we are never alone.
Kindness is the mortar, strong and true,
Binding us closer in all we do.

Amidst the storms that rage outside,
Within these walls, love will abide.
Sharing laughter, shedding tears,
Facing the world, confronting fears.

Through every challenge that comes our way,
In our fortress, we choose to stay.
For trust is the key to unlock the door,
To a safe sanctuary, forevermore.

As seasons change and years do pass,
Our fortress stands, steadfast as grass.
Built on kindness, a timeless blend,
Where hearts connect, and broken mend.

Embracing Change, Embracing Us

In every heartbeat, change takes flight,
Transforming shadows into light.
We stand together, hand in hand,
Embracing the journey, a new land.

With open hearts, we shed the past,
In waves of color, our sails are cast.
Letting go, we find our stride,
In every change, love is our guide.

The winds may shift, the paths may bend,
Through every trial, we learn to mend.
In the dance of life, we sway and twirl,
Embracing change, our spirits unfurl.

With every dawn, new hopes arise,
A canvas painted in endless skies.
Together we leap, uncharted ground,
In change we trust, our hearts are bound.

So let us cherish the twists and turns,
In the embrace of change, our spirit learns.
In every moment, both shy and bold,
We weave our stories, our futures unfold.

The Fire That Awaits in Every Season

Beneath the frost, the ember glows,
A promise of warmth that softly flows.
In winter's chill, hope may seem frail,
Yet deep within, desires prevail.

Spring's tender kiss brings bud and bloom,
Awakening dreams from winter's gloom.
With every petal that breaks the ground,
The fire within us is truly found.

As summer dances with vibrant light,
Passion ignites, hearts burning bright.
In sunlit days and laughter shared,
The warmth of love is fully bared.

Autumn whispers with a golden hue,
As leaves cascade, our spirits renew.
In every season, the lessons flow,
The fire within us will always grow.

Through cycles of life, we learn to see,
In every ending, a new decree.
With every moment, both rich and rare,
The fire that awaits is always there.

A Symphony of Hearts

In twilight's soft embrace we stand,
Two souls entwined, a gentle band.
The whispers of the night take flight,
A symphony of love ignites.

Heartbeats echo, rhythms collide,
Together in this timeless ride.
The music swells, it sweeps us high,
As constellations light the sky.

Each note a promise, sweet and true,
In every chord, I find my cue.
The world around us fades away,
In harmony, we choose to stay.

Through crescendos, soft and bold,
A love story forever told.
In every pause, we find our grace,
In this symphony, a warm embrace.

So let the echoes linger long,
In every heart, we share our song.
Together, dear, we'll play our part,
The sweetest tune—a work of art.

Perseverance of the Soul

In shadows deep where doubts reside,
A flicker glows, a steady light.
With courage forged through trials faced,
The spirit's strength cannot be erased.

Through storms that threaten, skies of gray,
Resilience blooms, a bright array.
Each hurdle met, a lesson learned,
In every heart, a fire burns.

For every tear that stains the cheek,
A story waits, profound yet weak.
In every fall, we rise anew,
The soul's resolve, forever true.

As mountains rise, we climb with might,
With steadfast hearts, we soar to heights.
The road may twist, the path unsure,
Yet through it all, we shall endure.

In the tapestry of life's grand scheme,
Each thread woven, a hopeful dream.
The strength within, a guiding scroll,
In perseverance lies the soul.

Embers of Our Journey

We walk along this winding road,
With every step, a story flowed.
The embers glow from fires past,
In memories, our shadows cast.

Through laughter shared and tears that fall,
Our hearts remain, we heed the call.
The echoes of our hopes reside,
In every moment, side by side.

Each turn we take, a lesson found,
In whispers soft, through silence sound.
The path ahead, though unclear still,
With courage drawn, we bend the will.

For every dawn that brings the light,
Is woven from the depths of night.
Together through the tempest's sway,
Our embers guide us on our way.

With hearts aflame, we'll chase the stars,
No distance wide, no fear of scars.
In every challenge, we ignite,
The embers of our journey bright.

The Language of Laughter

In joyful tones, our spirits rise,
A chorus bright, beneath the skies.
With every chuckle, every cheer,
We find connection, drawing near.

The playful jests, a dance of souls,
In shared delight, our laughter rolls.
A simple joke, a wink, a grin,
In every moment, joy begins.

In times of trials, laughter blooms,
A light that dances in the glooms.
It bridges gaps, it mends the strife,
The language sweet that hugs us tight.

Through echoes rich and hearty sounds,
We weave a bond that knows no bounds.
In every giggle, every tear,
The laughter sings—our loved ones near.

So let us share this joyful art,
A melody that fills the heart.
In laughter's rhythm, we rejoice,
Together singing—our own voice.

Seasons of Affection Unfolding

Spring whispers softly, blooms arise,
Love dances lightly under blue skies.
Summer's warmth wraps around our hearts,
With laughter and joy, the closeness starts.

Autumn leaves fall with a gentle sigh,
In amber hues, our spirits fly.
Winter's chill brings a cozy embrace,
In flickering light, we find our place.

Through every season, love's journey flows,
With tender glances and gentle prose.
Each moment cherished, a story to tell,
In the seasons of affection, we dwell.

Together we stand, hand in hand,
Facing life's storms, just as we planned.
With every heartbeat, our bond will grow,
In the ebb and the flow, forever we'll know.

As petals wilt, and frost may bite,
We find our warmth in each other's light.
Through seasons changing, our hearts remain,
In this love story, forever we'll gain.

The Art of Holding Hands

Fingers interwoven, a perfect fit,
In silent moments, together we sit.
A squeeze conveys what words cannot say,
In the art of holding hands, we find our way.

Every touch tells a story untold,
A canvas of warmth in the bitter cold.
The rhythm of life flows smooth and slow,
With hands clasped tight, we bravely go.

When doubts arise, and shadows creep,
Our joined hands promise, a bond to keep.
In laughter and tears, we find our stance,
In the dance of life, we share our chance.

Through crowded streets or quiet nights,
Hand in hand, we reach new heights.
In simple gestures, love blooms and grows,
In the art of holding hands, forever it shows.

So let us wander, across this land,
With strength in numbers, just as we planned.
In every moment, a joyous refrain,
In the art of holding hands, we'll always remain.

Embracing Imperfections with Grace

In every flaw, a tale unfolds,
A masterpiece crafted as life beholds.
With gentle hearts, we learn to forgive,
Embracing imperfections, we truly live.

Chipped porcelain, a beautiful sight,
Each crack tells a story, a dance in the light.
With open minds, we choose to see,
The beauty in scars, the gift of being free.

When shadows linger and doubts arise,
We gather our courage, lift our eyes.
In each errant step, there lies a grace,
A journey of love, in every space.

So let us celebrate our mismatched ways,
In life's grand tapestry, our hearts will blaze.
Hand in hand through trials and time,
Embracing imperfections, a rhythm, a rhyme.

As petals may fall, and colors may fade,
In every heartbeat, a promise is made.
With kindness and laughter to fill our days,
In embracing each flaw, love softly sways.

Enchanted by Everyday Moments

In the fluttering leaves, a whisper sings,
Nature's embrace, the joy it brings.
With sunrises painting the morning sky,
Everyday moments make our spirits fly.

A shared cup of coffee, warmth in our hands,
Conversations linger, as time gently stands.
The laughter of children, a sweet melody,
In everyday moments, pure harmony.

The rustle of pages, lost in a book,
Exploring new worlds, come take a look.
In the simple things, love can ignite,
Enchanted by moments, our hearts take flight.

Walking together through parks in bloom,
In every step, we find room to zoom.
Underneath the stars, our dreams take shape,
In the magic of night, we joyously escape.

So let us treasure each fleeting glance,
For in everyday moments, we find our chance.
To weave our story, both humble and grand,
Enchanted forever, hand in hand.

Heartbeats in Perfect Harmony

In quiet moments, hearts align,
A dance of souls, two stars that shine.
With every breath, the world turns slow,
In whispers soft, our true love grows.

The pulse of life, a shared embrace,
In every smile, a sacred space.
Together we weave a gentle song,
In perfect harmony, where we belong.

Through storms we've walked, hand in hand,
Our dreams take flight, like grains of sand.
With every heartbeat, I feel you near,
In love's sweet echo, I find no fear.

Each moment shared, a treasure rare,
In this quiet bond, we find repair.
With starlit skies above our head,
We paint a future where love is spread.

With every heartbeat, we start anew,
In this symphony, it's just us two.
Together we rise, as twilight fades,
In perfect harmony, love never strays.

Muted Colors of Shared Silences

In muted tones, our silence speaks,
A language soft, where comfort seeks.
The world outside fades into grey,
Within your gaze, I long to stay.

Gentle pauses, unspoken trust,
Our hearts entwined in the quiet rust.
In every sigh, a story told,
A tapestry of warmth, of bold.

The colors fade, yet love remains,
In stillness deep, we break the chains.
With every heartbeat, our souls combine,
In these quiet moments, you are mine.

Through shadows cast by fleeting light,
In shared silences, we find our might.
A world transformed in our embrace,
In muted hues, we find our place.

In the depths of night, we gently soar,
With words unspoken, we need no more.
In silent laughter, our spirits wake,
In shared silences, a love to take.

Love's Compass Pointing Home

In every journey, paths align,
With love as compass, we intertwine.
Through winding roads, our hearts can roam,
With every step, we find our home.

The stars above guide us at night,
In love's embrace, we find the light.
Each moment cherished, a map so clear,
With every heartbeat, I hold you near.

Through every storm and sunny day,
Your hand in mine, we'll find our way.
A safe harbor, where dreams take flight,
In love's warm glow, we chase the light.

In whispered prayers, our hopes ascend,
With open hearts, on love we depend.
No matter where the winds may roam,
In your arms, I always feel home.

As seasons change, our love will grow,
Through every tide, we'll ebb and flow.
Together forever, come what may,
In love's sweet compass, we'll always stay.

Bridges Built on Understanding

In every glance, a bridge we build,
In gentle words, our hearts are filled.
Through storms of doubt, we walk the line,
In trust and faith, our souls entwine.

With open minds, we share our dreams,
In laughter's glow, our spirits beam.
Each conversation, a path we pave,
Through kindness and care, we learn to brave.

In moments shared, we find our way,
With hearts unguarded, come what may.
Together we stand, side by side,
In understanding, love will abide.

Through fears and joys, we learn and grow,
With every story, our bonds will flow.
A bridge of love, forever strong,
In unity's grace, we both belong.

With open arms, we face the night,
In understanding's warmth, we find the light.
Together we'll rise, hand in hand,
On bridges of love, we'll always stand.